Watching the Weather

Rain

Elizabeth Miles

Heinemann Library
Chicago, Illinois

Customer Service 888-454-2279
Visit our website at www.heinemannlibrary.com

Designed by Richard Parker and Celia Jones
Illustrations by Jeff Edwards
Originated by Dot Gradations
Printed in the United States of America,
North Mankato, Minnesota

14 13 12
10 9 8

Library of Congress Cataloging-in-Publication Data
Miles, Elizabeth, 1960-
    Rain / Elizabeth Miles.
        p. cm. – (Watching the weather)
Summary: What is rain? – Where does rain come from? – Water in the air – The water cycle – Different kinds of rain – Rainfall around the world -- Rain and the seasons – Who needs rain? – Plants in the rain -- Animals in the rain – Floods – Acid rain – Project: rain diary.
Includes bibliographical references and index.
ISBN 1-4034-5577-5 (HC), 1-4034-5675-5 (Pbk.)
ISBN 978-1-4034-5577-2 (HC), 978-1-4034-5675-5 (Pbk.)
1. Rain and rainfall – Juvenile literature. I. Title.
QCp24.7 .M55 2005
                        2004002365

092012
006924

Acknowledgments
The author and publisher are grateful to the following for permission to reproduce copyright material: Alamy Images pp. 11, 16; Ardea/Ake Lindau p. 23; Corbis p. 6; Corbis/David Pollack p. 17; Corbis/Kevin Fleming p. 19; Corbis/Nick Hawkes; Ecoscene p. 27, Corbis/Raymond Gehman p. 13; Corbis/Sally A Morgan; Ecoscene p. 25; Corbis/William James Warren p. 5; Digital Vision p. 20; Getty Images/Image Bank p. 12; Getty Images/PhotoDisc pp. i, 22, 26; Getty Images/Stone p. 4; Harcourt Education Ltd/Tudor Photography p. 28; PA Photos/EPA pp. 18, 24; Panos Pictures/Sven Torfinn p. 21; Robert Harding Picture Library Ltd p. 7.

Cover photograph of rain falling on grass reproduced with permission of Corbis/Craig Turtle.

Every effort has been made to contact copyright holders of any material reproduced in this book. Any omissions will be rectified in subsequent printings if notice is given to the publisher.

Contents

Some words are shown in bold, **like this**. You can find out what they mean by looking in the glossary.

What Is Rain?

Rain is water that falls from the sky. Rainwater can make us wet and make puddles on the street.

We wear raincoats and carry umbrellas on rainy days.

Rain is made up of many drops of water.
These are called raindrops. You can see
raindrops when they stick to the outside of
a window.

Where Does Rain Come From?

When we see a lot of clouds in the sky, we know it might rain.

Rain comes from clouds. Clouds are made of billions of tiny drops of water called **droplets**. Droplets are so small and light, they float in the air.

When water droplets join together they get big and heavy. Soon they get too heavy to float in the air. Then they fall from the clouds as raindrops.

Water in the Air

When the Sun heats water on the ground, some of it rises into the air. It rises as a **gas** called **water vapor**. We cannot see water vapor in the air.

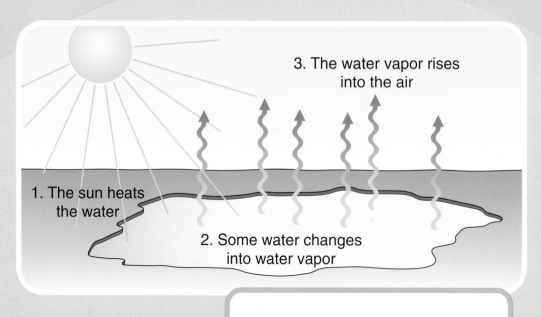

3. The water vapor rises into the air

1. The sun heats the water

2. Some water changes into water vapor

The way that liquid water changes into a gas when heated is called **evaporation**.

When water vapor rises high in the air, it cools down. It becomes tiny **droplets** of water again. The droplets form clouds in the sky.

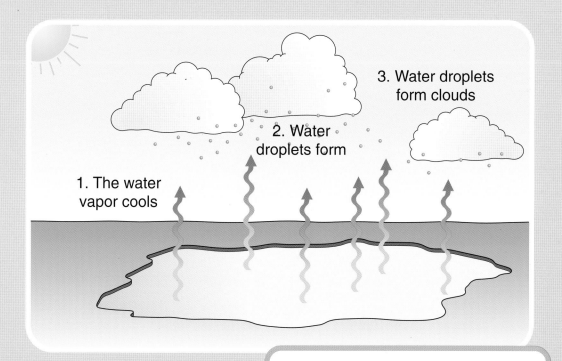

3. Water droplets form clouds

2. Water droplets form

1. The water vapor cools

The way in which water vapor changes into water droplets is called **condensation**.

The Water Cycle

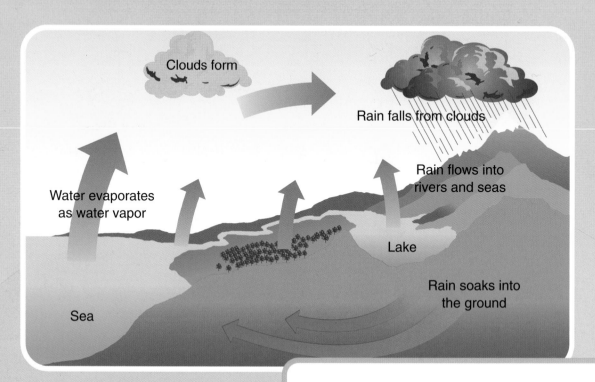

Clouds form

Rain falls from clouds

Water evaporates as water vapor

Rain flows into rivers and seas

Lake

Rain soaks into the ground

Sea

Water is moving through the water cycle all the time.

Rain is part of the water cycle. The water cycle is the way water keeps rising into the air as **water vapor** and falling again as rain.

In the water cycle, rain falls onto the land and into the sea. It fills rivers and lakes. Some rain soaks into the ground. It joins all the other water around us.

Rain runs into rivers. Rivers take rainwater to lakes and the sea. All this is part of the water cycle, too.

Different Kinds of Rain

Raindrops can be small or large. Small raindrops make drizzle or light rain. The raindrops in drizzle can be as tiny as bits of dust.

Even the small raindrops in drizzle can make us wet.

When raindrops fall
on water, they make
round patterns.

Sometimes many large raindrops fall.
This is called a downpour or heavy rain.
Raindrops in a downpour can be bigger
than peas.

Rainfall Around the World

This map shows how much rain falls over a year, in different parts of the world.

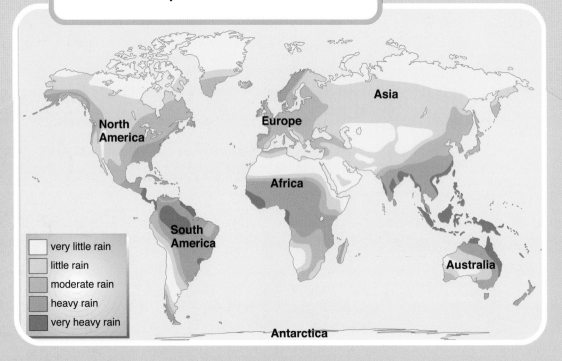

- very little rain
- little rain
- moderate rain
- heavy rain
- very heavy rain

North America

Europe

Asia

Africa

South America

Australia

Antarctica

The amount of rain that falls in a year is called the annual rainfall. In some parts of the world, there is a lot of rain. In other parts, there is hardly any rain.

Rain can fall in a special way near mountains. When wind blows up a mountainside, it cools down. **Water vapor** in the air turns to rain. By the time the air blows down the other side of the mountain, it is dry.

The dry side of a mountain is called the **rain shadow**. Little or no rain falls here.

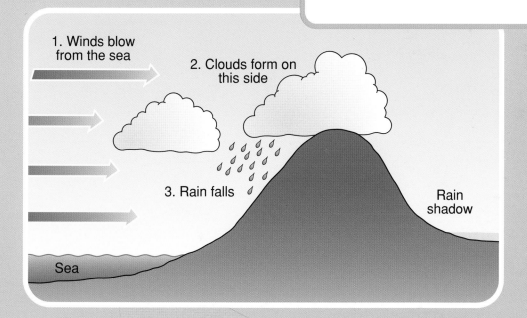

1. Winds blow from the sea

2. Clouds form on this side

3. Rain falls

Rain shadow

Sea

Rain and the Seasons

Many places have two seasons: a dry season and a rainy season. In the dry season there is little or no rain. The rainy season brings plenty of rain.

People are often happy when the rainy season starts, because it means the end of a long, dry hot season.

In winter, sometimes the air is so cold that **snow** falls instead of rain.

Some parts of the world have four seasons: winter, spring, summer, and fall. It can rain in any season.

Who Needs Rain?

Everyone needs rain to stay alive. Rain brings the water that people drink. People also need rain to grow **crops**.

Many people around the world eat rice every day. Rice needs a lot of water to grow.

Water in reservoirs is cleaned before it is pumped through pipes to your home.

When rain falls to the ground, some of it drains into **reservoirs** and lakes. The water in your faucets probably comes from a reservoir.

Plants in the Rain

Plants need water to live. Many plants grow in places where there is plenty of rain. Thousands of plants grow in the **rain forests** of South America.

A lot of rain falls in rain forests such as this. Trees here can grow higher than a ten-story building!

When a place does not get enough rain for a long time, it is called a drought. Many plants can die in droughts. If **crops** die, people may have nothing to eat.

A farmer has nothing to sell when his crops die in a drought.

Animals in the Rain

Just like people, animals need rain to live. Many animals leave their homes when there is no rain. They travel a long way to places where they can find water.

Many animals gather to drink at pools of water, such as this one in Africa.

Slugs come out to feed on plant leaves after it has rained.

Some animals need the damp weather that rain brings. Slugs need to keep their bodies wet. In dry weather, they hide under the ground.

Floods

Rain can cause floods. When a lot of rain falls in a short time, rivers can fill up. The rainwater then spills out over the land.

People trapped by a flood might have to climb onto the roofs of cars or houses to escape.

These houses are high off the ground to protect them from floods.

In parts of Asia, heavy rain often causes floods. Some houses are built on wooden legs called stilts. This means that they are safer when the floods come.

Acid Rain

Rain that carries **pollution** is called acid rain. Most of the pollution comes from factories and power plants. It mixes with **water vapor** and makes acid rain in the air.

Pollution from factories mixes with the air.

Over several years, this stone wall has been worn away by acid rain.

Over time, acid rain can damage stone buildings and statues. Acid rain can also fall in lakes. This can spoil the water for the fish, so they become ill or die.

Project: Rain Diary

Find out how much rain falls where you live. To measure rainfall you need a rain gauge. This is how you make one.

1. Ask an adult to help you cut the top off the drink bottle.
2. Take the bottom part of the bottle and use a ruler to draw a line up the outside.
3. Add small marks every half inch up to six inches along the line. This is your rain gauge.

4. Dig a small hole in the ground outside. Stand the rain gauge in it.

5. Put the top part of the bottle upside down in the gauge. This will help collect the rain.

6. Check the bottle each day. Write down how much rain is in it. Then empty out the water.

7. Look at your rain diary after a week. Which day had the most rain?

There is about two inches of rain in this rain gauge.

Glossary

condensation when water changes from a gas (water vapor) to a liquid

crop plant that farmers grow for food, such as vegetables or rice

droplet very small drop of a liquid, such as water

evaporation how water changes from a liquid to a gas (water vapor)

gas does not have a solid shape and cannot be poured like water. The air is a gas.

pollution smoke or dirt that can damage the water, land, and air around us

rain forest thick forest that grows in hot, rainy places

rain shadow dry side of the mountain that does not get much rain

reservoir lake where water is stored

snow water droplets in clouds that turn from liquid to solid and fall to the ground

water vapor water that is part of the air. Water vapor is a gas that we cannot see.

More Books to Read

Ashwell, Miranda and Andy Owen. *Rain*. Chicago: Heinemann Library, 1999.

Flanagan, Alice. *Rain*. Eden Prairie, Minn.: The Child's World, Incorporated, 2003.

Hughes, Monica. *The Water Cycle*. Chicago: Heinemann Library, 2004.

Royston, Angela. *Water*. Chicago: Heinemann Library, 2001.

Index